Dream Catcher

BEHIND THE POEMs

Dream Catcher

BEHIND THE POEMs

Sukrita

Vani

Vani

4695, 21-A, Daryaganj, New Delhi 110 002

Branch

Ashok Rajpath, Patna 800 004

Phone : +91 11 23273167 Fax : +91 11 23275710

www.vaniprakashan.in

vaniprakashan@gmail.com
editorial@vaniprakashan.in
sales@vaniprakashan.in

DREAM CATCHER
by Sukrita

First Edition 2014
Second Edition 2016

ISBN : 978-93-5072-759-1

Poetry

Cover Photograph permission arranged by Manish Pushkale

Price : ₹ 100

Printed at Yash Printographics, Noida-201 301 (U.P.)

Vani Prakashan's signature motif is created by Artist Maqbool Fida Husain

Preface

This little book offers an exercise in self-reflexivity, as a sort of loud thinking on what lies behind my poems. The "Other" and "I" are two chapters in the book, that present two sides of the same mind. They reach out to each other and yet each functions on its own. In the writing of these chapters, I leave them both behind to move on to fresh pastures...

Sukrita

to

lal ded, akka mahadevi, andal...

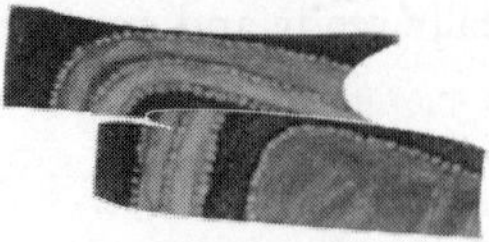

Other

The blank sheet stares back at me in defiance each time I sit to write a poem. My eyes are dazzled with the white of the sheet and I remain in a stupor wondering when, if any, words will flow from the fingers waiting on the keyboard. Each time some poem is ripe and I believe "ready" in my head - and my heart heavy with it - a compulsion to deliver urges me to confront the blank sheet...but then, the slow pain of deliverance has to be gone through! Soon enough I realize, it's a poem in the making and not really ready and complete in the head. The right expression calls for deliberation. The frozen whiteness has to melt into a warm throb of life...the black words forming lines, one nestling towards the other. Close, far, some lines more far. The size and shape right. Just right for the lines to wriggle closer to the trigger...to take off for a fresh journey. Black upon white, not battling but negotiating difference and contrast. The space, in writing over it, gets sucked into the poem, becoming the content itself. Measured emptiness of space, getting ready to speak the language of the poem.

Life within life dancing on
Feather feet
The rising belly, a tight sponge
Puffed into lightness.

For the poem to come to be, it is crucial to catch the delicate vibrations of sound waves emanating from the empty space, not through perked up ears but the skin of the body - like that of a snake. This sound of silence can be felt only as the right words find their place on and around the empty spaces. And here is where the heart of the poem throbs …when I am able to hear it loud and clear, I take courage to slip off the trodden paths of my mind to go into the wilds in search of some unknown truth. There is a studied play of words, sounds and space. I urge all words to vanish into their sounds and merge into the total experience of the poem.

In the forest
no one is lonely;

green parrots,

bits of my soulful past

swinging from tree to tree

taking sprightly flights
and showering messages

of yore in the hues

of the present

But then what is it that compels me to take the challenge and sit in front of the blank sheet to create a new world? Why the arrogance of being the creator? I know I am not God. My fingers tremble when I write this because I am completely conscious of those moments of utmost humility – and even embarrassment at times, when no words come to mind - when I sit down to write! A strange sense of emptiness and yet compulsion, grips one…there is always that huge chasm- between what is shaping up in the mind and the writing that has yet to happen. Either I am flooded with too many words or then, have none at all to express what I want to! I get petrified because I might fall into the chasm headlong and get totally annihilated but then, if I take courage and dive deep into the ocean I sometimes manage to locate some hidden treasure in those specs of sand, each one carrying its own universe…

Talking of sand reminds me of the Tsunami scenes on the television and in newspapers that had turned the earth topsy-turvy with each day throwing up gory images.

Hanging like a coconut,

The head stuck between the

Branches of

a half broken palm tree

The little boy

on the

lonely planet

saw water below

swelling

with corpses.

Words had to be tenderly and carefully used if only to capture the intuitive experience of Tsunami and also perhaps to release it from the confined domain of *personal* experience, to go out there to some "other"!

I realized that there was this "other" in me, always seeking expression, motivating me to recognize her and demanding her space within my consciousness. I can rarely dismiss her compelling call. Whenever I write poetry, I know I am responding to her, contacting her and re-establishing-as it were-my faith in her. She is extremely observant, and sometimes she draws my attention towards herself very noisily. Specially if I am talking to someone, she suddenly wants to capture me and that, I confess, can be very disconcerting. My eyes betray my sudden absence from the conversation.

That can be very embarrassing. The dilemma is that while I may seem to dismiss her, I am in fact always looking for ways to attend to her. Each of my poems is actually the result of an appointment with her ... with someone who cannot remain confined to prescriptive behavior and social decorum. Frankly, I don't want to tame her. Whenever I have tried to do that, my poetry becomes a starched stiff doll unable to laugh or cry naturally. Sometimes she emerges winking and dancing fearlessly in her naked honesty but at times I have to labour hard to give her a natural skin, flesh and bones. Each time, her birth is as much an agony as the happiness of the delivery of a new born. I feel a sense of absolute familiarity with her but at the same time, also a total strangeness with the new face it acquires in each poem! She is both my unborn as well as the born babies. I have no choice but to rear her, for my own survival really. I'd be lost without her. I'd be poisoned with her death within me.

What I write depends on where I might hear her, feel her or even smell her. I find her at times sitting on top of a branch of a tree or inside the rugged trunk; she might just breathe life into a dead political news-item in the newspaper or she may peep from the eyes of an infant in the arms of a mother. She could be the voice of hunger of the abandoned woman on the road…a lingering whisper from my grandmother who died feeling a fugitive! She could even be the cheer in the wings of a bird ready to fly…

Ironically words themselves get used to make the poem wordless. Only echoes of sounds and the feel of the experience may remain... the poem is not to conclude in meaning but to remain in search for some revelations within the poet and then the reader. Meaning is easy to ferret out but for the creative process to lead to a revelation one has to agonize, fly, fret, fall and rise many times over!

A poem can make the mountains move and tame the virulent waves, but in itself it needs to have a still core. The frenzy of the spirit of writing a poem must get translated into a perfect poise, that of movement and apt punctuation through line or stanza breaks, commas etc within the poem. These are the moments of reflection as well as relief that get the birds to fly out of the cages…

Swimming in deep waters

I drown again

And yet again

But come afloat always

At times the poem decides to become a painting and the pen dips as a brush into the mindscape of colours.

Picking the blue of the skies
from one end,

Offering it to the other…

When I wished to make a painting of the Chinese doing Tai chi at dawn in the Hong Kong park, I wrote the above lines just so that I'd remember the visual for a painting later. But the result was a weaving of a poem around these very lines. In fact, many a poem of mine has been born out of an image or a colour. The "colour" white became the inspiring source for a series of little poems, "Winter Poems at Minnesota". Here's one of them:

Black snow on the road

Is treacherous

as the white night

At full moon
Snow flakes float in mid air

Looking for the ground

To settle or

Melt away

My favourite Korean poet, Ko Un said somewhere "I want to lie in my grave writing poems." Inherently, I believe, each one of us is by nature a poet but external forces work against this "primeval" reality and the poet inside is gradually throttled into being a non-entity. Given half a chance, this poet-self lying crouched in some corner of one's self, is ready to awaken and explore life afresh. And, if one is able to shake out of standardized or the rather clichéd frames of living, the force of creative energy takes over…To be able to take such a path- though fraught with all kinds of hazards – promises the unraveling of life-secrets totally invisible otherwise. If one has opened one's mind to these forays and has tasted creative thrills, as Ko Un says, how can one wean one's self away from it all even after death,

It has to emerge

On this vacancy

From the black holes

Of the universes, seen and unseen,

Through meteor storms and

Somersaulting planets

The hand has to appear with

The finger pointing

This way

That way

In the process of writing a poem, I have often felt the "I" in myself slowly diminishing and some other unseen hand taking over, leading the poem and taking it towards some end… an illusion of an end that is really just another beginning!

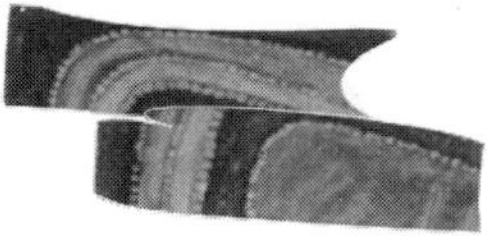

I

Right from my infanthood as I was growing up, the words have echoed in my ears constantly, *"We have to go back home."* And of course when we came to India... we would come for a holiday and took sea journeys. And it used to take us 8 to 10 days each side. The following poem must have been lived over and over again as I took those voyages with the family as a child:

Voyaging at Ten

Between awesome expanses

of deep blue oceans

and the greying sky

I stood

a speck in God's creation

leaning on the rails

of the deck

sailing from Mombasa

to Bombay...

a journey with a

beginning and an end

and no middle

A storm

a swarm of sharks

or whales

failure of

the engines of Amra

or a mere giving way

of the railing

Blue death;

Anything,

a trivial something

or a grave lapse

I cannot swim

The shores are not

in sight...

I cannot forget those journeys. Travels....yes, but the pertinent point is that in my childhood I missed getting a sense of home, and when at sea I identified so much with the physical experience of "shorelessness"! Different shades of blue, the big and tiny waves, the silver fish taking small flights and splashing little fountains of water ... I remember staring at all of that for hours as I stood on the deck of the boat...The blue of the ocean at times merged with the blue of the skies while I searched for the line of horizon. I don't know how many poems could have actually emerged out of that emptiness or, I wonder, are they still lying in my subconscious, waiting to be unveiled through my pen or brushes?

In my nightmares in sleep as also in my wakefulness, for years did I carry the conflicting, irreconcilable shadows of my grandmother Bhabhoji within myself. It was only after I relived my past and re-visited different layers and folds of my relationship with my grandmother, that I began to feel somewhat free of that peculiar tension. It was like finding her warm lap all over again...or, was it actually locating a freedom from it, a freedom to fly on my own, higher and unattached! I don't know. All I can say is that I have felt lighter ever since, and as the Portuguese writer Jose Saramago put it, "on the seismograph of my soul" no more did I record any tremors of the kind I had constantly experienced earlier.

Often have I wondered why I did not write a poem about my intense relationship with my grandmother; why did I write the story, "Visitation", instead? It is interesting to see how the following poem may serve as a preface to that story:

Connections

Thank you, Amma

for the moon, thank you

I had stood

stretched

longer than my life

stiff on my toes

heels aching

heavy

with the unexpressed

seeking

the silver moon

carrying a million

in its orbit

Greetings to you

my dear

for walking out of

childhood dreams

for unfreezing

those wrinkles,

shedding tears

and smiling,

rising with the new sun

a lease of life

not an illusion

nor a trap of compassion

a mirage in the golden sands,

firm-edged love

twinkling through

round spectacles

with copper rims

food for the starved

Thank you Amma

for carrying the cross

our cross

vibrating on your lean body

through so many homes

and alleys, backlanes

and galis

in transit

always

stepping in and out

of dreams

all those

moons and stars

toss and turn

in the universe

waiting for you, Amma

to connect them

with us

sleepwalking

on the earth

Looking back, I realize that this poem too visits the same domain, that of the strange bonding I had with my grandmother. The poem stands on its own, independent of the story but evokes the same memories!